© 1996 Geddes & Grosset Ltd

Reprinted 1997

Published by Geddes & Grosset Ltd,
New Lanark, Scotland.

ISBN 1 85534 172 7

Printed and bound in the UK

A^BC

Judy Hamilton
Illustrated by Beverley Sprio

Tarantula Books

Aa
Apple

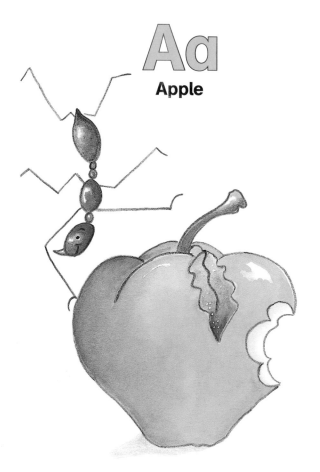

Aah! There's **an** **a**nt on my **apple**!
He's quite **an** **a**crobat!

Bear

Belinda the **bear b**ounces **b**y with her
big **b**lue **b**all.

Cc
Cat

Clara the **c**at eats **c**arrots to **c**ure herself of her **c**old and **c**ough.

Dd
Dog

Douglas the **d**og **d**ozes in the **d**oorway, **d**reaming of his **d**inner.

Ee
Elephant

Ernest the **elephant** gets his **e**xercise **e**very day, juggling **e**ggs.

Ff

Fish

Fish can't play **f**ootball.
Fish have **f**ins, not **f**eet!
Not **f**air!

Gg
Goat

Gus the **goat** plays in **g**oal on the **g**reen.
Go, **G**us, **g**o!

Hh

House

Hattie's **house** is **h**alfway up the **h**ill.
Hattie's **h**ouse is **h**uge!

Ink

Indian **ink** is **i**mpossible to wash out.
Invisible **ink** is **i**mpossible to see.

Jj
Jack-in-the-box

James has **j**ust bought a **jack-in-the-box** at the **j**umble sale. **J**ust look at it **j**ump!

Kk

Kite

King **K**evin is flying his **kite**.
Keep it up, **K**evin!

Ll

Lion

Leonard the **lion l**ounges in the **l**ong grass after **l**unch. **L**eonard sleeps **l**ike a **l**og!

Mm

Mouse

Mary the **mouse** found a **m**uffin.
"**M**m! **M**arvellous!" she **m**umbled
as she **m**unched.

Nn

Nurse

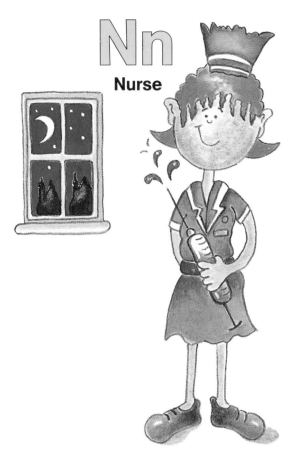

Nancy the **nurse** works at **n**ight.
Nancy is **n**ifty with a **n**eedle!

Octopus

Oliver is no **o**rdinary **octopus**.
Oliver is **o**range!

Pp
Penguin

Percy **Penguin p**osed by the **p**ool
in **p**urple **p**yjamas.

Qq
Queen

The **queen** felt **q**ueasy as she waited in the **q**ueue. **Q**uite **q**uietly, she left.

Rr
Rabbit

Robert **Rabbit** **r**an **r**ather well in the **r**ace.
But **R**achel **r**ushed past him and won.

Ss
Seaside

Sausages get **s**lightly **s**andy if you **s**izzle them at the **seaside**!

Tt
Tiger

Tigers can get **t**erribly **t**etchy if you **t**read on **t**heir **t**oes!

Uu **Umbrella**

Uh-oh! Rain!
Up with your **umbrella**!

Vv **Violin**

Vincent plays the **violin**
in his **v**est.

Ww
Winter

Wear your **w**oollies to keep yourself **w**arm!
Winter can be **w**indy and **w**et!

Xx  X-ray

Look at your bones in an **X-ray**!
Look for **x** in words like fo**x** and bo**x**.

Yy Yacht

Have **y**ou seen a
yellow **yacht** like
this one?

Zz
Zebra

Zebedee looked after the **zebras** in the **z**oo.
Zebedee wore a jacket with a **z**ip.